Usborne
A Doodle a Day

Tear-off pad

Words by
Phil Clarke

The doodlers wh[o]

Michael Hill

and

Laura Hammonds

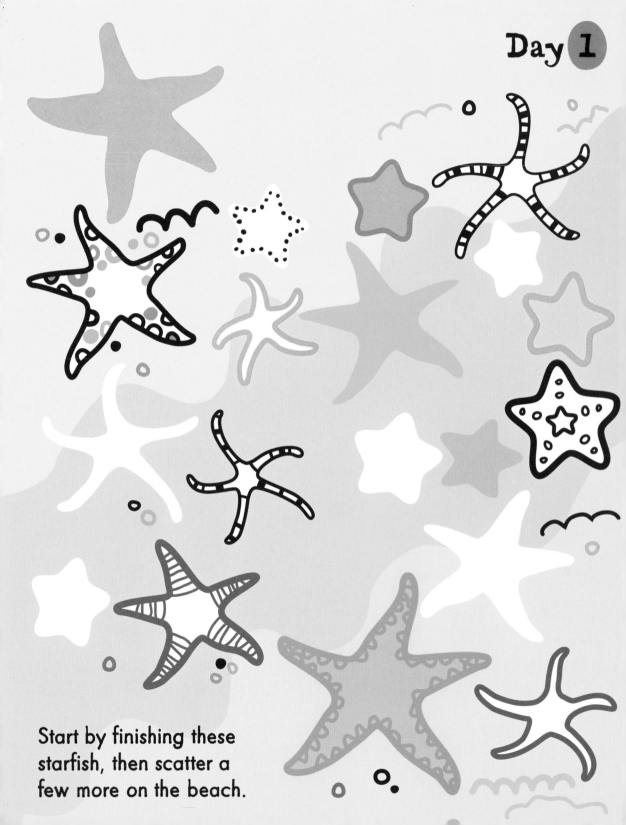

Start by finishing these starfish, then scatter a few more on the beach.

Day 2

Add some more leaves growing on this tree,
and tumbling off it in the wind.

Day ③

Doodle all kinds of
patterns inside the circles.

Give these sheep thick, woolly coats, and finish their faces too.

Today, fill the plate with a generous helping of spaghetti and meatballs.

Complete the butterflies, and decorate their wings with pleasing patterns.

Doodle the astronauts' faces and spacesuits, and design the flag.

Add more rooms, towers and chimneys to this house.

Complete each
picture as you like.

Day 10

Add more details
to the giraffes
and give them
leaves to munch.

Today, doodle
more knitwear and
winding wool.

See how many different patterns
you can doodle on these stripes.

Today, the world's greatest masterpiece will be unveiled.
It's a picture of you, as doodled by – you!

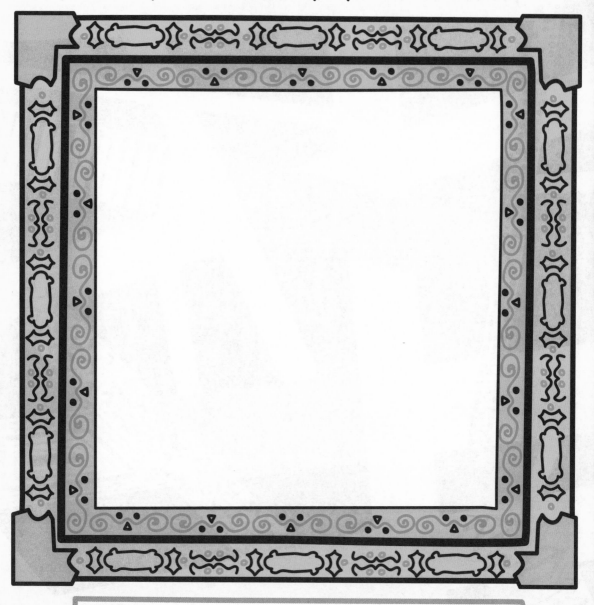

Self-portrait by: ....

Turn each of these inkblots into something much more interesting.

Today's doodle is doggy faces and muddy pawprints.

Scatter a few
more leaves on
the forest floor.

Day 17

Today, turn these simple squiggles into super-doodles.

Doodle some faces on your family tree.

Ali Baba's cave is full of treasure, but there's room for more.

Laughing clowns,
crying clowns...
finish all the faces.

Doodle ridges, teeth and scales on these lazy crocodiles.

Let the mountains stretch as far as the eye can see.

Day 23

Doodle more little trains on this page.

Doodle some skiers today. Don't forget the trails they've made too.

Day 25

Fill the page with
overlapping doodles.

Day 26

Add more vehicles and design the signs.

Day 29

Deck out these boards with daring doodles.

SKATE

Add more stitches, patches, buttons and embroidery.

What would you love to take with you to a tropical island?

Doodle designs for these stained glass windows.

Make the garden bloom today with lots of little leaves and flowers.

Rumble! Crash! Boom! Add raindrops, hail and lightning to this stormy sky.

Maybe cave paintings are just prehistoric doodles? Add more hunters, animals and decorations.

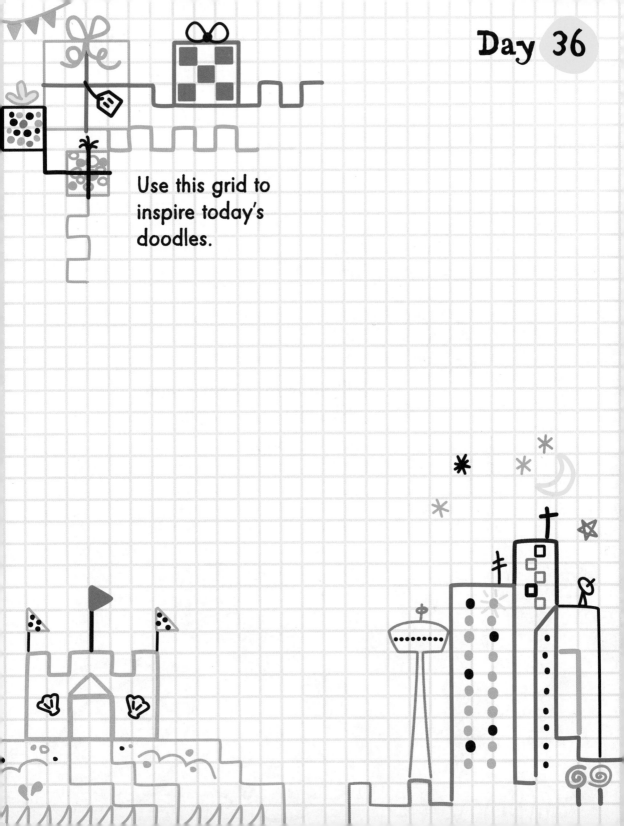

Use this grid to inspire today's doodles.

Fill the leafy garden with silhouettes of creeping, buzzing bugs.

Continue the scribble,
then fill it with doodles.

These frames are looking a little empty.
Fill them with fun pictures.

Doodle the ice creams of your dreams, with all the sprinkles and toppings you like.

Day 41

Add the finishing touches to these towering skyscrapers, and build a few more.

Doodle the other
half of each picture.

These animals need faces. Doodle them in.

Today is the perfect day to build a treehouse, don't you think?

Decorate these doughnuts
with yummy toppings and
sugary sprinkles.

DOODLE ST.

BUTTERFLY FARM

Where do you want to go today? Doodle some destinations on the signposts.

All these elephants need a drink, but some also need faces, tusks and toes.

The key to this doodle is to doodle
as many keys as you can.

Animal? Vegetable?
Mineral? Doodle
more objects in
circular patterns.

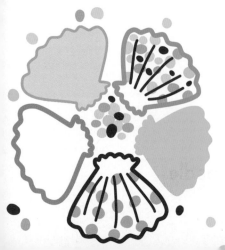

Reach for the skies today, as you doodle decorations on these kites.

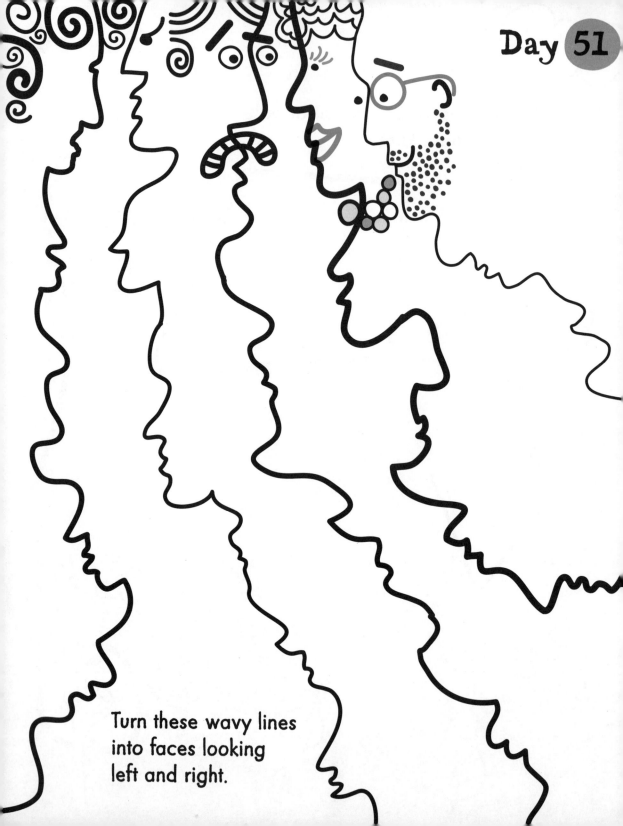

Turn these wavy lines into faces looking left and right.

Add more clutter to the shelves of the garden shed.

Draw doodles on
top of doodles on
top of doodles...

Finish these fine feathers.

Fill this page with
sporty doodles.

Add antlers,
eyes and ears
to the deer.

Continue the doodle outward from the middle.

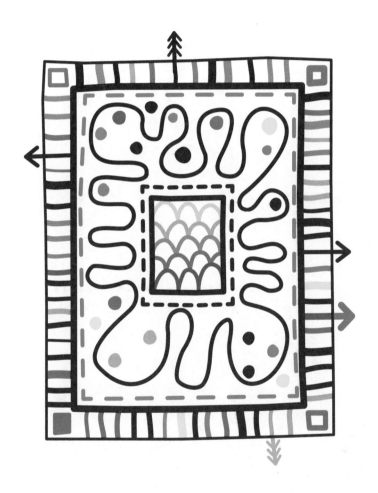

Like any celebrity, you need a star for your dressing room door.
Add your name, and some starry doodles to show your style.

Cut or tear along this dotted line →

Very Important Person

Doodle details on the trees and houses, and add a few more.

Look around you, and
doodle whatever you
can see right now.

Decorate the boats
and doodle waves
lapping at their sides.

How many more impossible things can you doodle?

We're on the SUN!

HELLO!

For today's doodle, give these monster trucks some style and attitude.

Decorate the dragonflies' delicate wings.

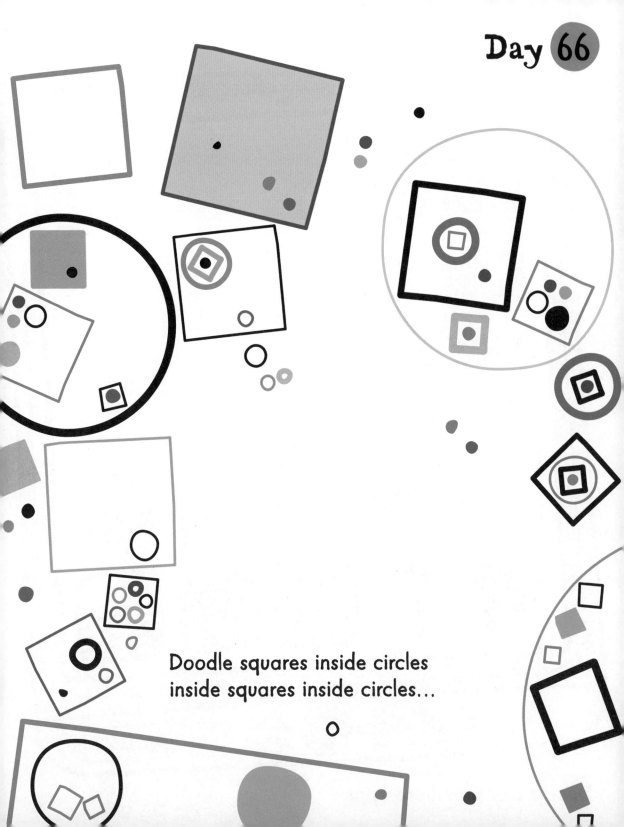

Doodle squares inside circles
inside squares inside circles...

Doodle icons for these apps.

Today's challenge is to doodle in the spaces using only straight lines.

Doodle more busy bees
making beelines
through the air.

Design more patterns on this triangular grid.

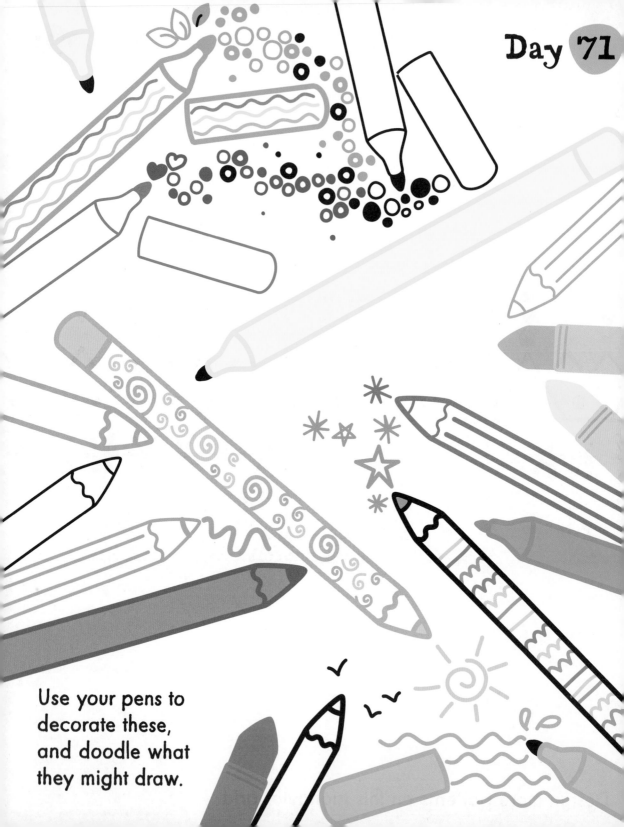

Use your pens to
decorate these,
and doodle what
they might draw.

The flowers are bursting with fluffy seeds – doodle more petal patterns, seeds and bugs.

Today, doodle in and around these overlapping squares.

Doodle in the gaps to complete the story.

O NCE UPON A TIME, there was a little

who lived inside a . Although he was small,

he was very brave. One day, a

attacked a nearby town. The people were terrified, but

the little hero and saved the day.

The people were so grateful

that they rewarded him with a

Spruce up these pots and hanging baskets with shrubs and flowers.

Add some expressions to this faceless crowd.

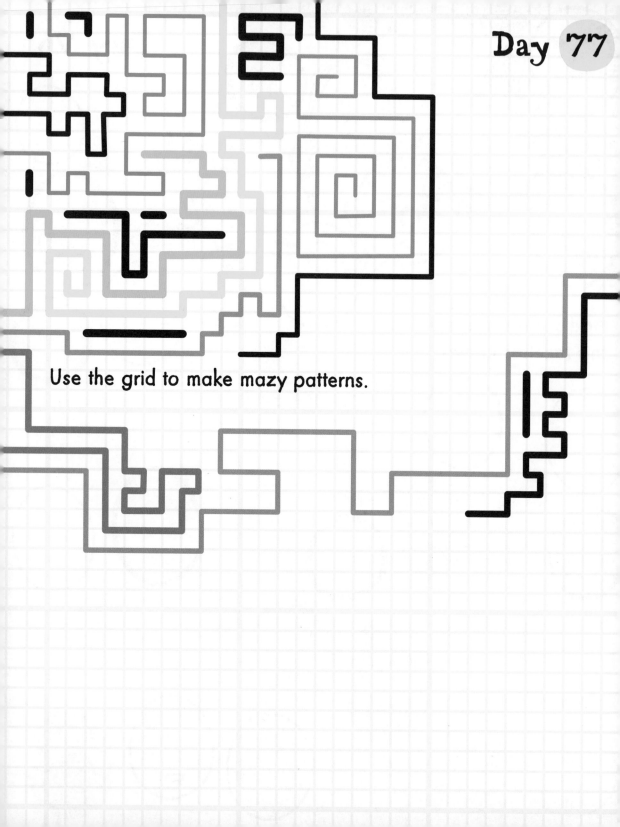

Use the grid to make mazy patterns.

Complete the rocket trails with smoke and flames, and doodle a strange, alien trail for the flying saucer.

Today is Hexagon
Day! Decorate them
with lavish designs.

Doodle chicks
and hens, and
add leaves to
the bushes.

Complete this cabinet of gleaming trophies.

1st

WINNER!

Add sparkly patterns to the horses and carousel.

Add more windows, turrets and flags to this fairytale castle in the clouds.

Fill every circle with a doodly design.

Fill this page with spinechilling doodles – if you dare...

Use this grid to inspire your doodles today.

Make these bubbles into a
crowd of funny faces.

Jazz up these boots with your stylish designs.

Write your name in large letters, decorated in your own style, to make a sign for your room.

Cut or tear along this dotted line

Continue this pattern using straight lines only.

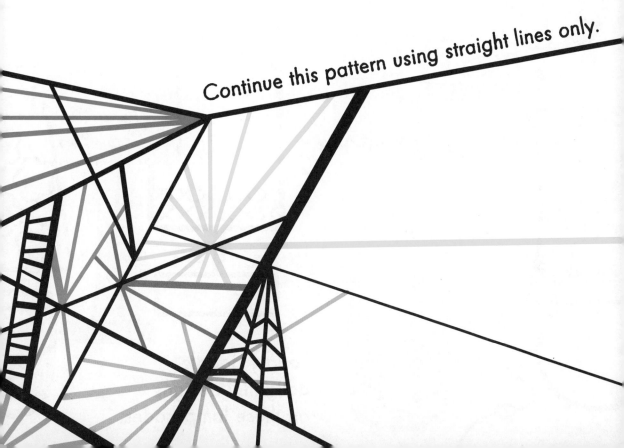

Today, doodle
delightful designs
on these lampshades.

Fill the page with more buttons and twirling threads.

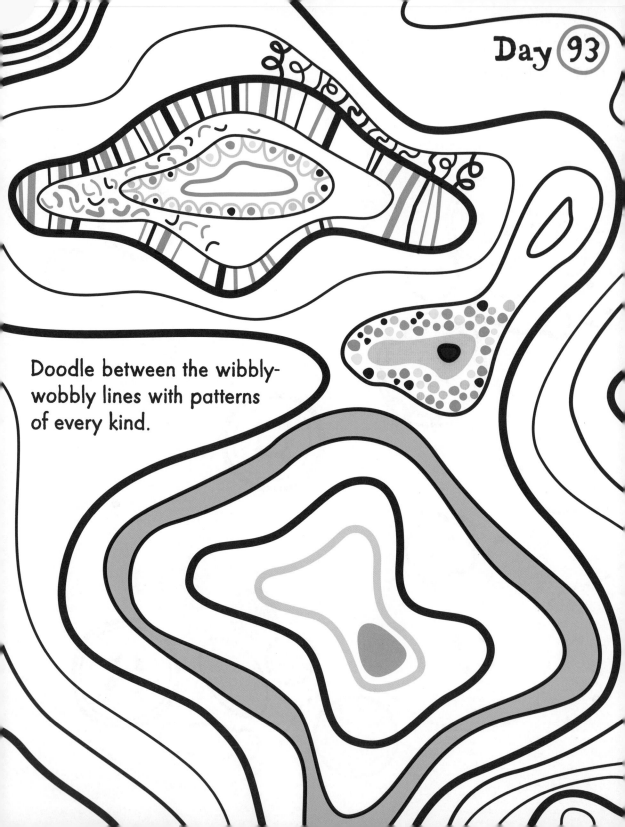

Doodle between the wibbly-wobbly lines with patterns of every kind.

Day 94

Invitation
to a Pirate Party
for

Rail Ticket
from:
to:

Remember to:
on:
at:

Busy, busy, busy...
fill this notice board
with notes, memos
and doodles.

Complete the spiders and
their webs, and bring
some bugs for dinner.

Decorate these presents with some snazzy giftwrap.

FOOD

Round and round and round – use the circles to create doodles.

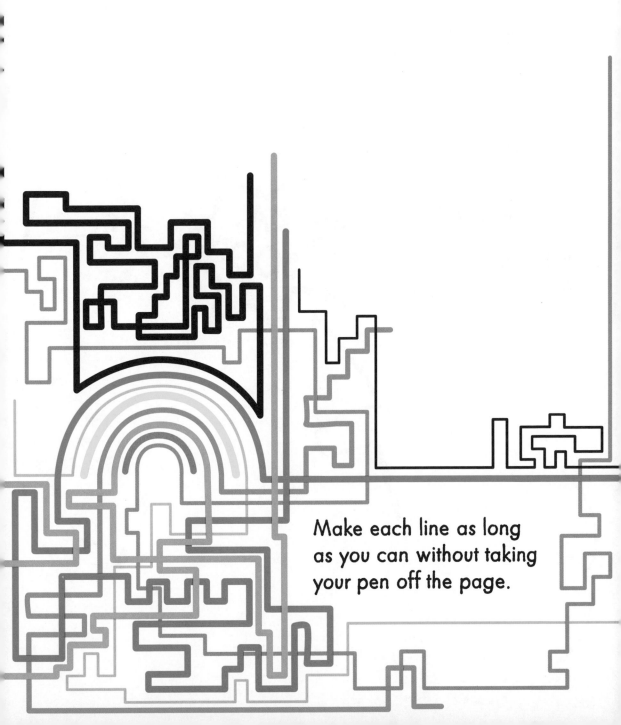

Make each line as long
as you can without taking
your pen off the page.

KA-BOOM

Fill the sky with whizzing rockets and exploding fireworks.

You've found the pot of gold at the end of the rainbow. Doodle more coins, and gems and other glittering treasures.

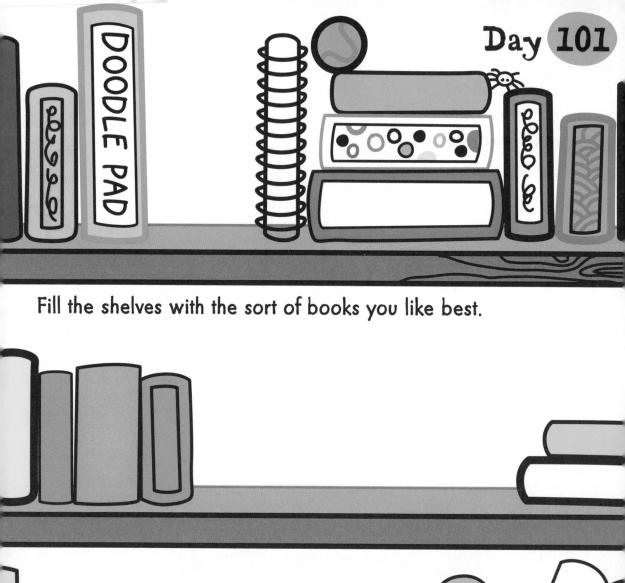

Fill the shelves with the sort of books you like best.

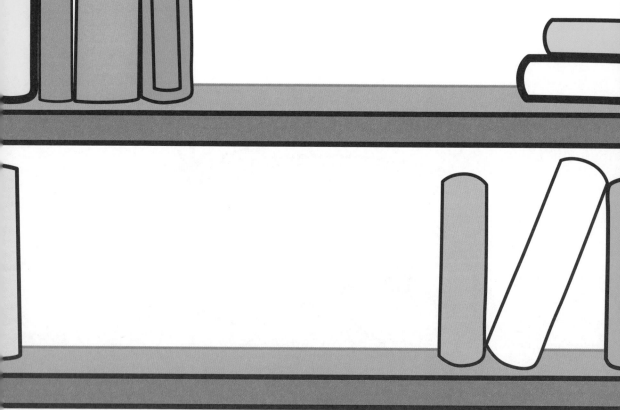

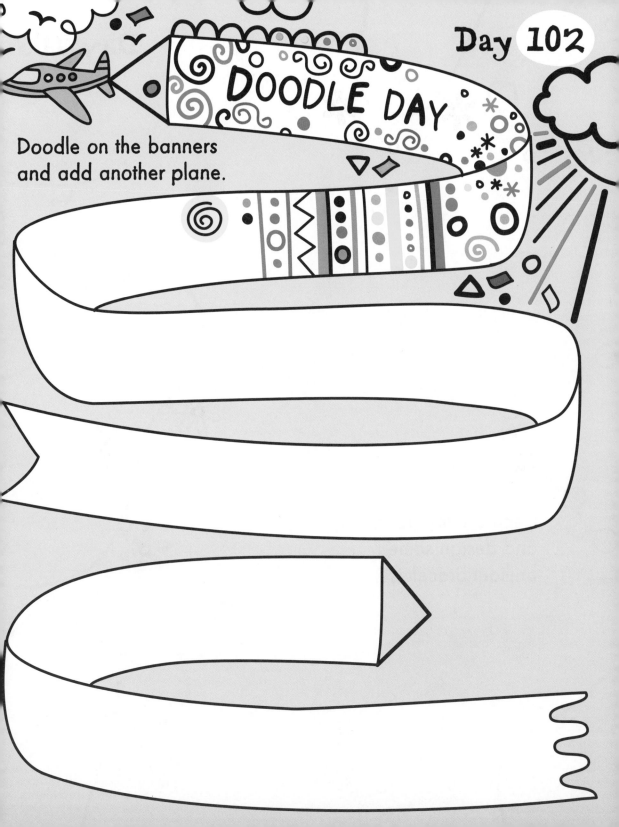

DOODLE DAY

Doodle on the banners
and add another plane.

Decorate the beads
and design some
brilliant bracelets.

For your doodle today, give these exotic lizards eye-catching patterns.

Doodle some more portraits for this gallery.

What could each shape become?

What do you see in the waves today? Doodle away...

Design starry patterns on this grid.

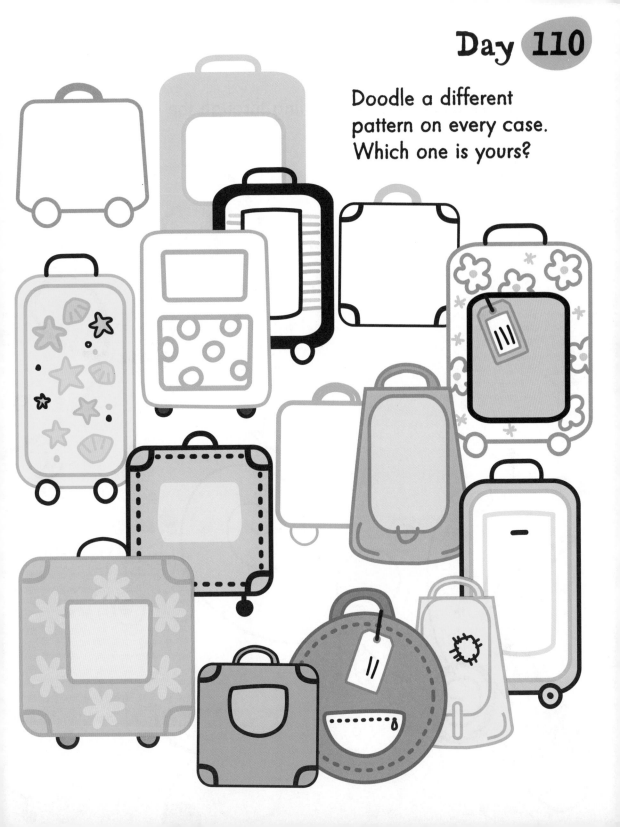

Day 110

Doodle a different pattern on every case. Which one is yours?

Doodle more musical notes swirling through the air.

What do you see in the clouds?
Turn them into anything you like.

Turn these eggs into a crowd of faces.

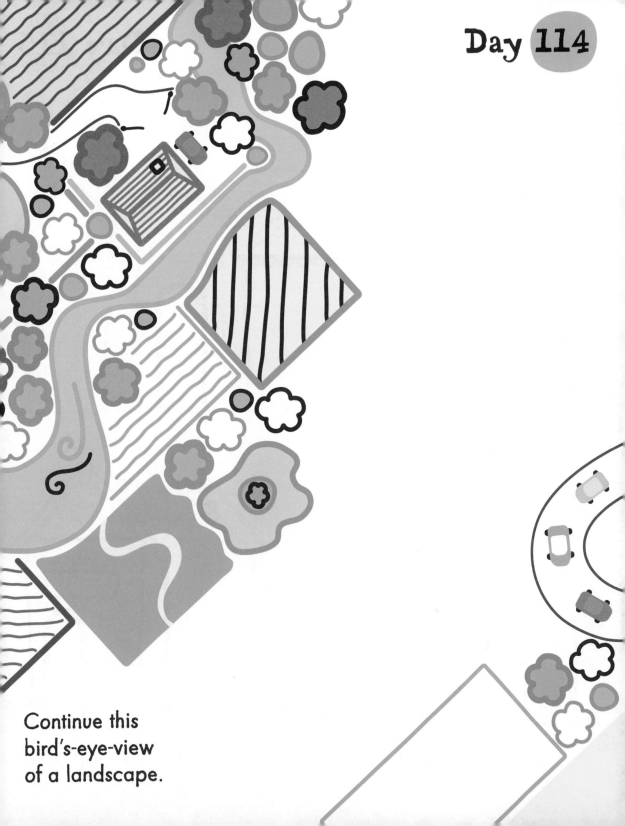

Continue this
bird's-eye-view
of a landscape.

Improve these beach huts
with cheerful decorations.

Doodle a message
made of letters cut
from magazines.

Decorate the domes and spires of this Middle-Eastern city.

Give each fan a
different pattern.

Day 119

Today, turn these blobs into doodle animals.

Fill the page with lollipops, candy canes, and other sweet treats.

Complete this tentacled
team of octopuses,
jellyfish and squid.

Doodle on the bird houses, and add more bugs, birds and leaves.

Let doodle-covered hills stretch away to the horizon.

What else will appear out of the magician's hat?

Complete the crabs, and doodle some more – but make it snappy!

Woooooooooo! Fill the page
with ghosts and ghoulies.

SURPRISE

Use this boxy grid to build your doodles.

Add doodly decorations
to spiral seashells today.

Today, finish off these jellyfish with twirling tentacles and jolly faces.

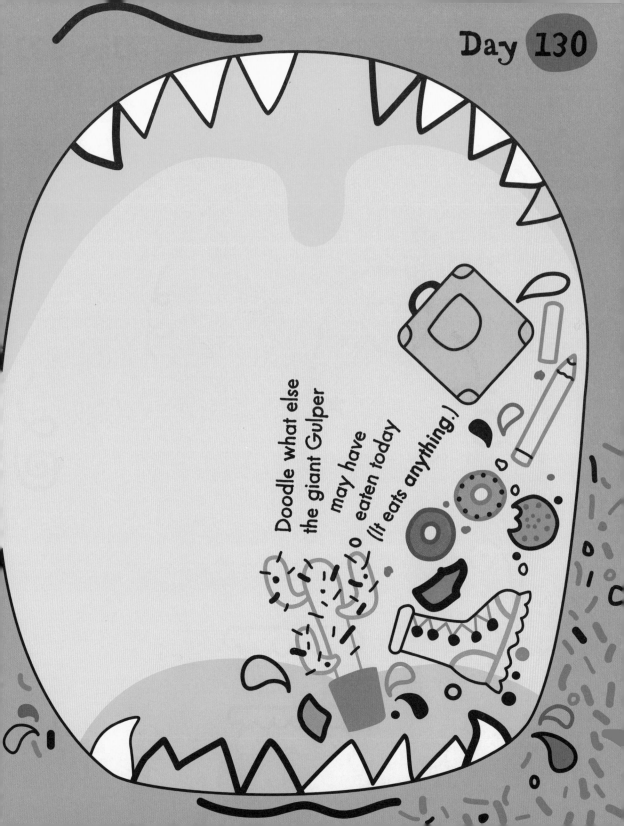

Doodle what else the giant Gulper may have eaten today (It eats anything!)

Fill the air with water spraying from the fountains.

Decorate these cakes,
and doodle a few more.

Add patterns to
these trendy tents,
and flowers to the field.

INCOMING CALL

Decorate these smartphones and doodle some screensavers.

Continue these spirals, then fill them with decorative doodles.

See if you can give every piece of the patchwork a pattern of its own.

Use this diary to imagine your life in doodles.

today:

tomorrow:

the day after:

this week

Day 138

Fill these snaky lines with all sorts of doodly shapes.

Carve a few more hieroglyphic
doodles in this ancient tomb.

Day 140

* Give these owls faces, feathers and ear-tufts.

In today's doodle, design a
looping, swerving rollercoaster.

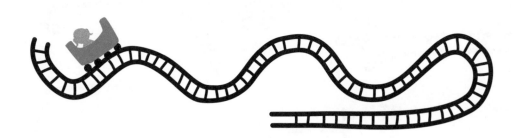

Complete the little pictures.

Doodle faces and patterns on the Russian dolls.

Day 144

Snakes alive!
Doodle patterns
on their skin.

See how many different shapes and patterns you can make using only triangles.

Make starry patterns
that twinkle and sparkle.

What will you do with all these semicircles?

MEOW

Doodle more of the
countless stars that you
can see through the telescope.

Print your own designs on these T-shirts.

It's DOODLE DAY!
Design some
cards to celebrate.

Add ripples, swirls and droplets to the waterfall.

Doodle what you think creatures living on Mars might look like.

Turn each
footprint into
something else.

Make each caterpillar
as different as you can.

Today's doodle is absolutely anything and everything that you like. On your marks, get set – doodle!

my best mate

Bob

Hello, my name is...

Doodle patterns on the lollipops,
then add an icy delight of your own.

Doodle the other halves of these pictures.

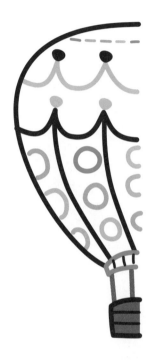

Who or what will you doodle peeking out of these windows today?

Today, why not decorate these cookies and gingerbread people?

Add spots, stripes and twinkly stars to the decorations.

Doodle patterns of your own
stretching across the page.

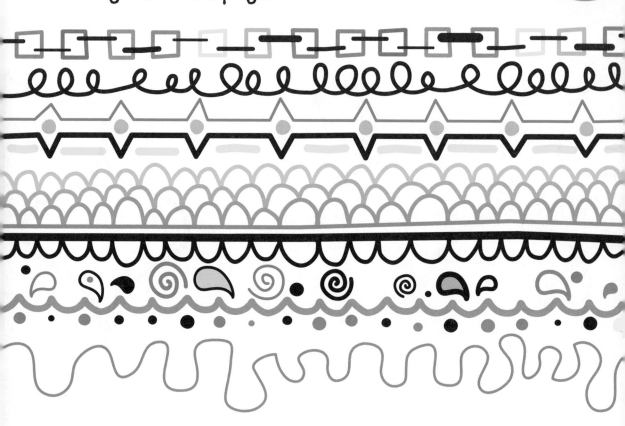

How many more bats can
you doodle flapping
into this cave?

Add patterns to these socks, but be sure to doodle matching pairs!

Do you ever feel like someone is watching you? Doodle more eyes.

See if you can join up the twisty, turny roots to make one giant tangle. Add a few more bugs too.

Fill the box with yummy chocolates.

Add more pieces to the jigsaw puzzle, and others scattered around.

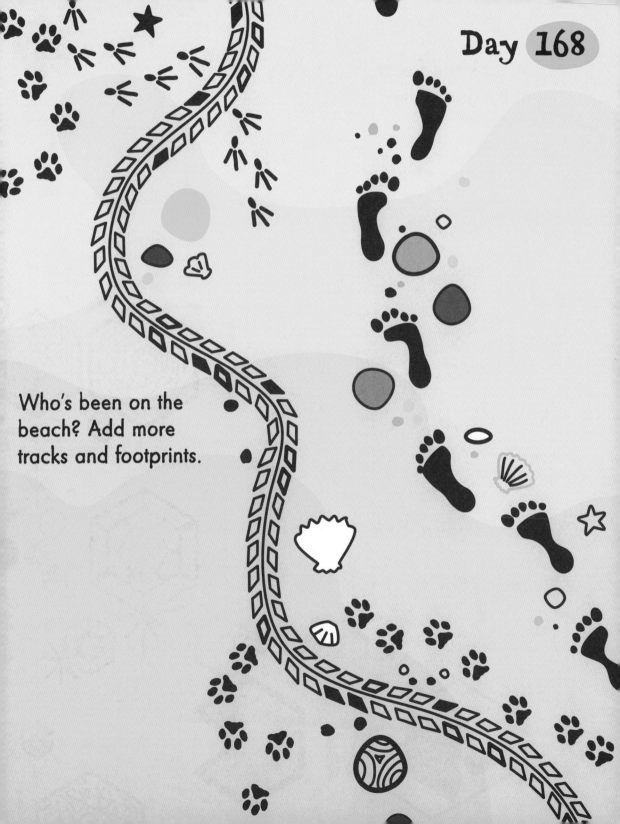

Who's been on the beach? Add more tracks and footprints.

Try out some freestyle doodling on this grid of hexagons.

Day 169

Design some gloves today.

Turn each fingerprint
into a different doodle.

Give each pumpkin
a grimace or a grin,
and doodle more.

Embellish these wooden masks with eye-catching designs.

Turn this blizzard of dots
into a world of doodles.

Finish these robots with bolts, rivets, lights and dials.

Add your own doodly style
to these paisley patterns.

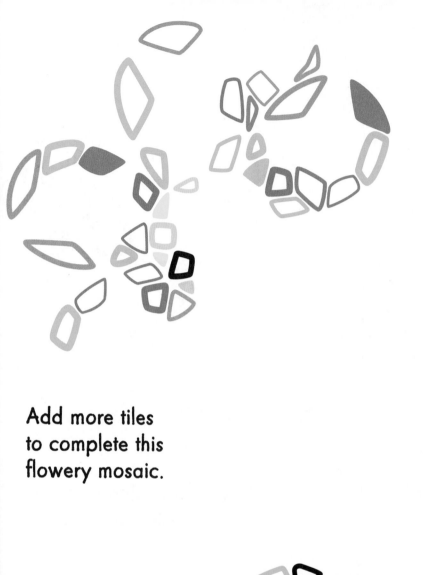

Add more tiles
to complete this
flowery mosaic.

Doodle the things you like...

...and the things you don't like.

Brighten up these umbrellas with your designs.

Stare into the crystal ball. What doodles will appear inside?

Fill the page with patterns of circles and flowers.

Day 182

Add more bricks to the wall, and cover it in patterns.

Today, bring these numbers to life with your doodling skills.

Fill the sea with plenty of fabulous fish.

Today, finish off these birds by doodling details of your own.

Complete this comic strip with pirates, flags and hungry sharks.

Add some royal sparkle to these crowns with gleaming gems and precious stones.

Fit doodly patterns into
these shapes and lines.

Decorate these surfboards
with awesome designs.

Design some key rings to show what you're crazy about.

I've been to the bug museum

i ♥ cakes

Bring these paper chain people alive.

Today's doodles all have a point.
See how many types of arrows
you can fit on this page.

Doodle lots of cogs
with intermeshing teeth.
Can you work out
which way each
one would turn?

Draw another cactus or two, and add plenty of prickles.

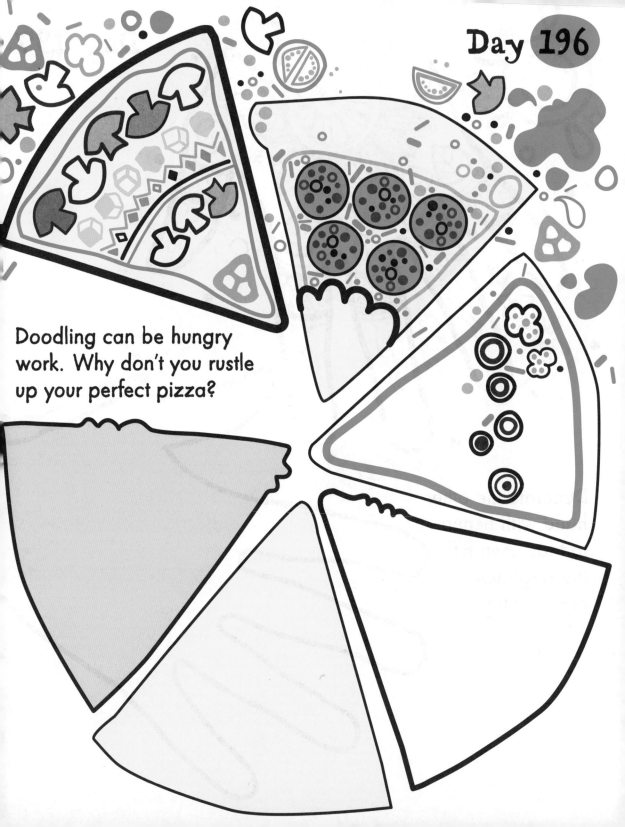

Doodling can be hungry work. Why don't you rustle up your perfect pizza?

Decorate the other hand with henna tattoos, then fill the page with more patterns.

Doodle these scarves into woolly wonders

You're in a secret cavern deep below the ground.
Add more sparkling gems and huge, glittering crystals.

Make these cookies look even more delicious with a topping of doodles.

See how many different things you can make from these squares.

Today, plant some more vegetables in the garden.

DOODLE O'S

Give all the groceries names and doodle a label for each one.

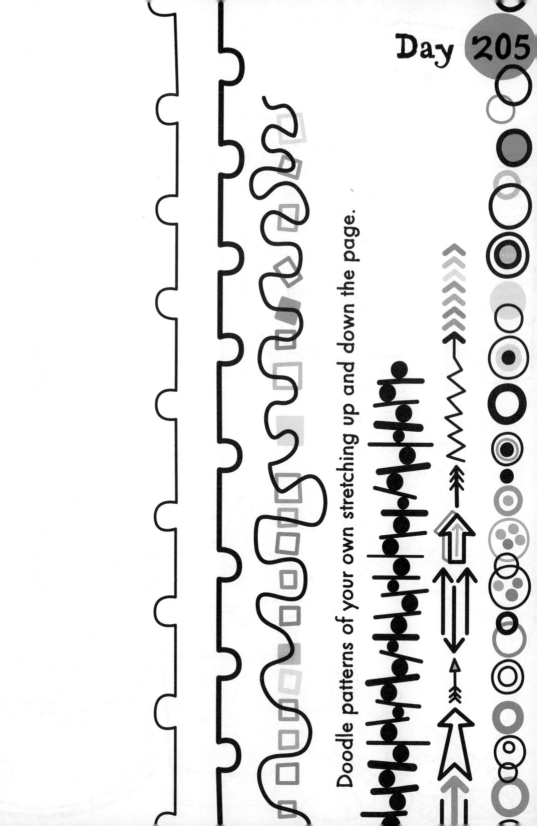

Doodle patterns of your own stretching up and down the page.

Add patterns to the turtles' shells, and doodle more fish.

Doodle houses, cars, trees and rivers on these rolling hills.

Put patterns inside these shapes
and borders around them.

Finish doodling these street signs.

Give these witches different faces
so you can tell which witch is which.
Add horrible hairdos and pointy hats.

These seaside doodles are all made with one long line. Create some more.

What patterns
do you see in the
stars at night?

What will the aliens beam up into their flying saucers?

Give these books eye-catching designs, and titles to match.

How to drive... Tractors

my palm tree stamp

Complete this scrap book page with doodles and details of your own.

the doodle

Today, you're at a balloon festival. Add some more patterns and names to the hot-air balloons.

Decorate the cover of your book for Doodle Class.

NAME

·······································

CLASS

·······································

SUBJECT ·· Doodling ······················

Decorate the cake for a great celebration.

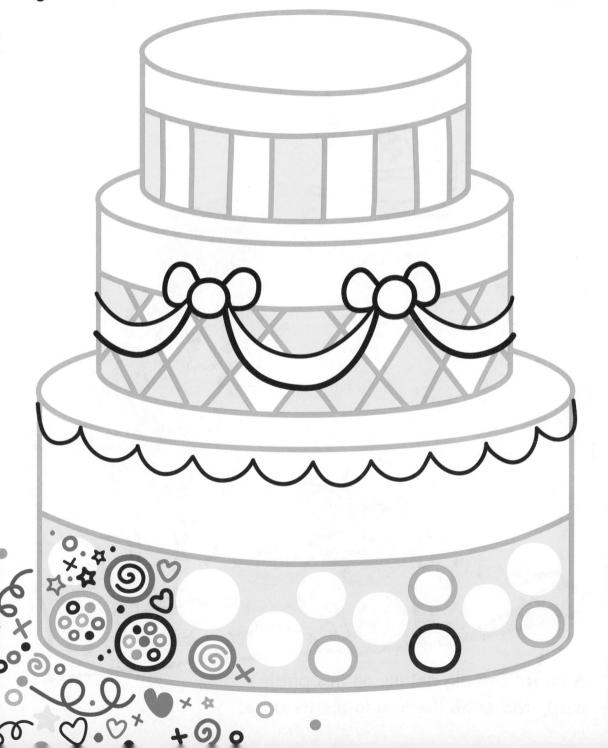

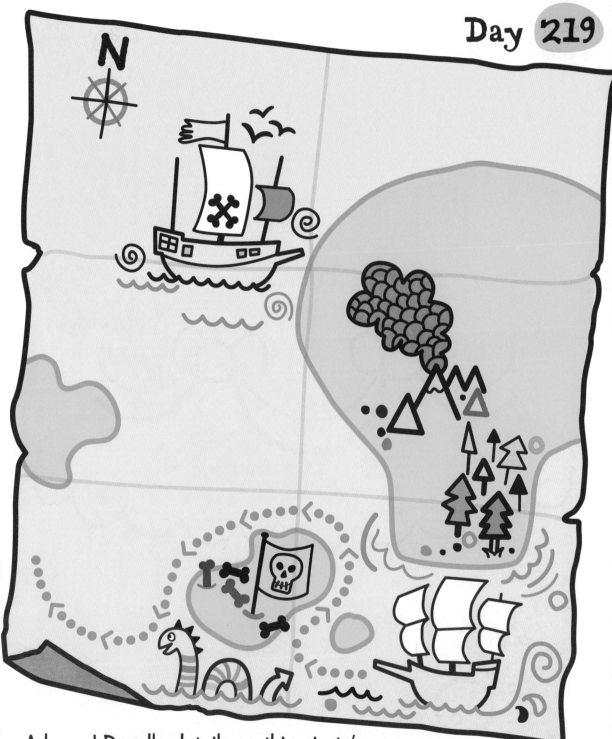

A-harrrr! Doodle details on this pirate's map, and finish the trail to the treasure.

Let the plates overflow with food,
and don't worry about the mess!

Without lifting your
pen from the page,
see how long each
doodly line can be.

Day 222

Cram as many patterns
and shapes as you can
into this swirly design.

Have fun in the sun
doodling your own
beach towel designs.

Doodle what the tornado is blowing away.

Dragon fight! Fill the page
with fierce and fiery doodles.

Design some doodles to make these ads more appealing.

HOUSE FOR SALE

Two-bedroom house with stunning views of bus station. One careful owner and hardly any ghosts.
Call 01-2-000000

DOG FOR SALE

Much-loved pet has outgrown house. Likes juicy bones and small children.

DOODLER

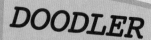

Freelance doodle-monkey. Will work for peanuts. See some examples of my recent work below!

EVERYTHING MUST GO!

It's finally here — our LAST EVER closing down sale! It's even better than last time!

GOING CHEAP!
Contact Ernie ASAP on 241-442-844

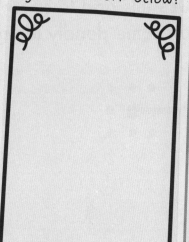

Use this grid to spark
off some doodly ideas.

Help the sheriff track down these crooked cowboys by doodling their faces and filling in their names and crimes.

Is there someone you want to thank? Here's your chance...

Cut or tear along this dotted line

Dear ....

Thank you!

Day 230

Dress the snowmen and finish their faces.

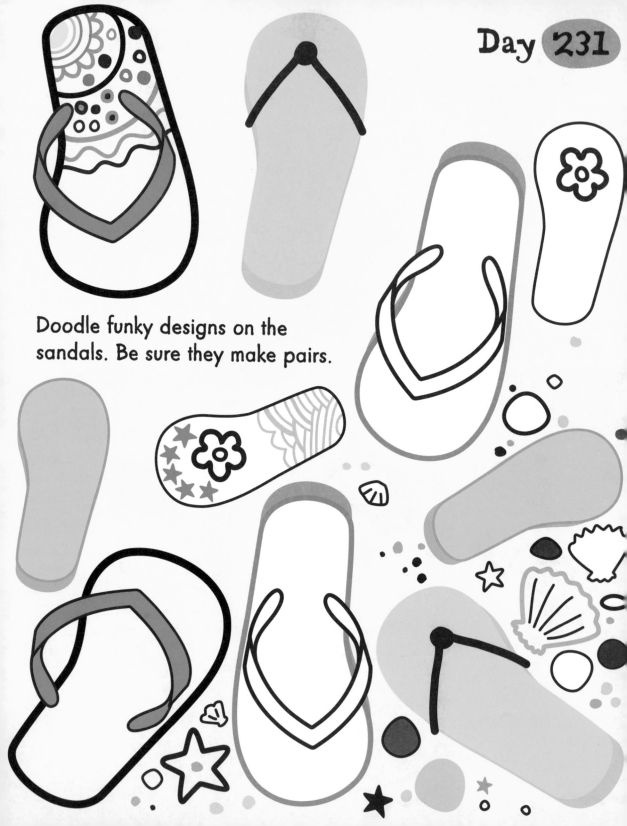

Doodle funky designs on the
sandals. Be sure they make pairs.

Today, see how
many different
patterns you can
doodle in the grid.

Doodle what you might see at night with a flashlight.

Doodle a list to remind you of the things you need to do today.

Put plenty more penguins on the icebergs.

Day 236

Doodle + Doodle =
brand new doodle!
Try it here...

Decorate these yo-yos with whizzy designs.

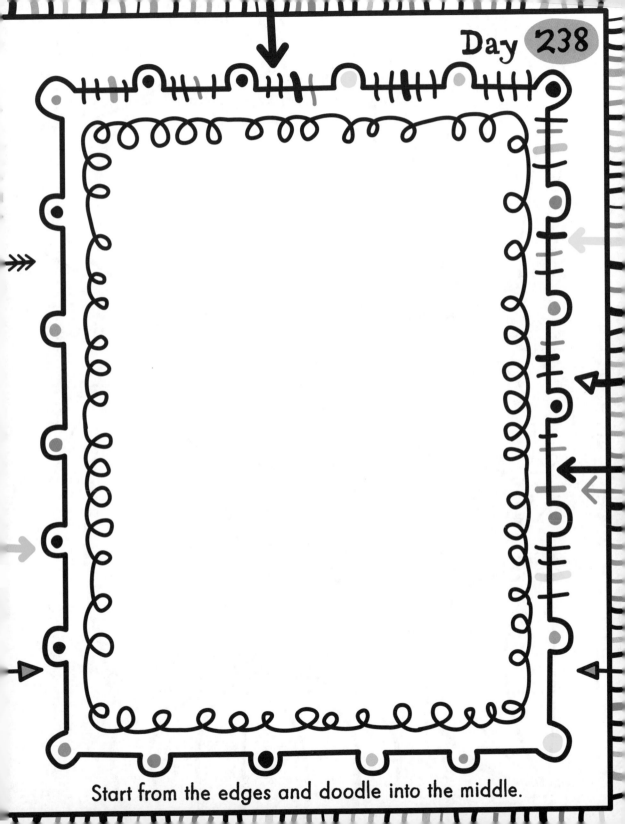

Start from the edges and doodle into the middle.

Paper lanterns for you to decorate...

Doodle extraordinary patterns on these zebras.

Fill the sky with swirling
snowflakes and wintry whirls.

Doodle a face on the scarecrow and give his clothes more patches and stitches.

Add jolly patterns
to these balloons.

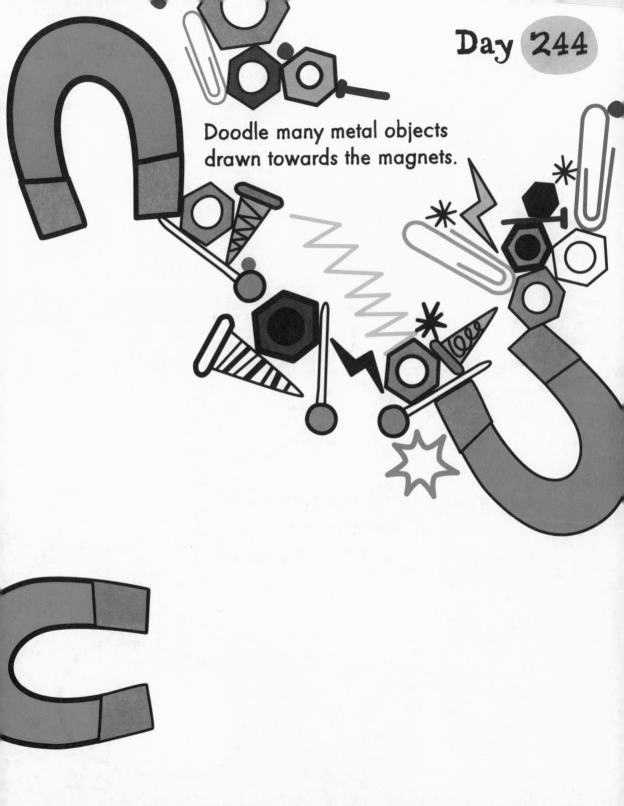

Doodle many metal objects drawn towards the magnets.

Big beasts and little critters – make them as monstrous as you can!

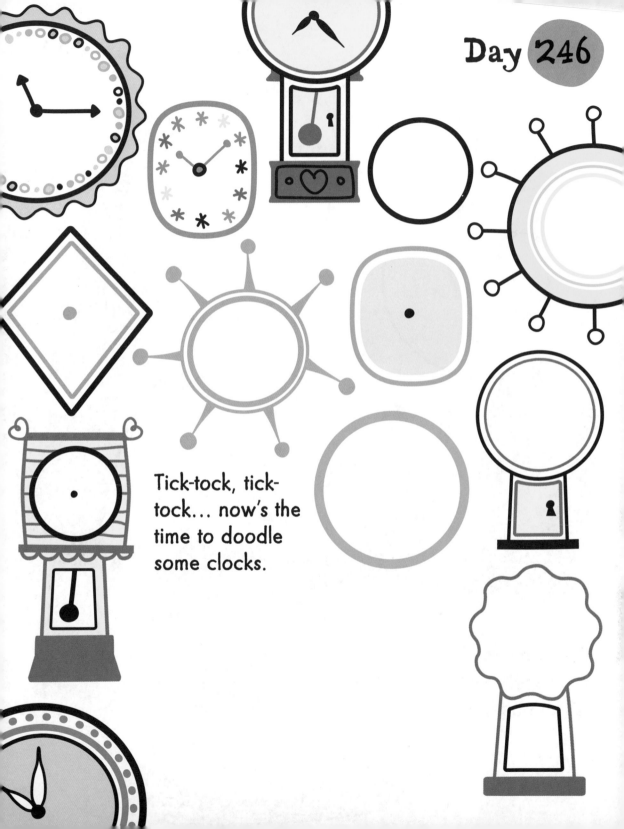

Tick-tock, tick-tock... now's the time to doodle some clocks.

Decorate the
snail shells with
spiral patterns.

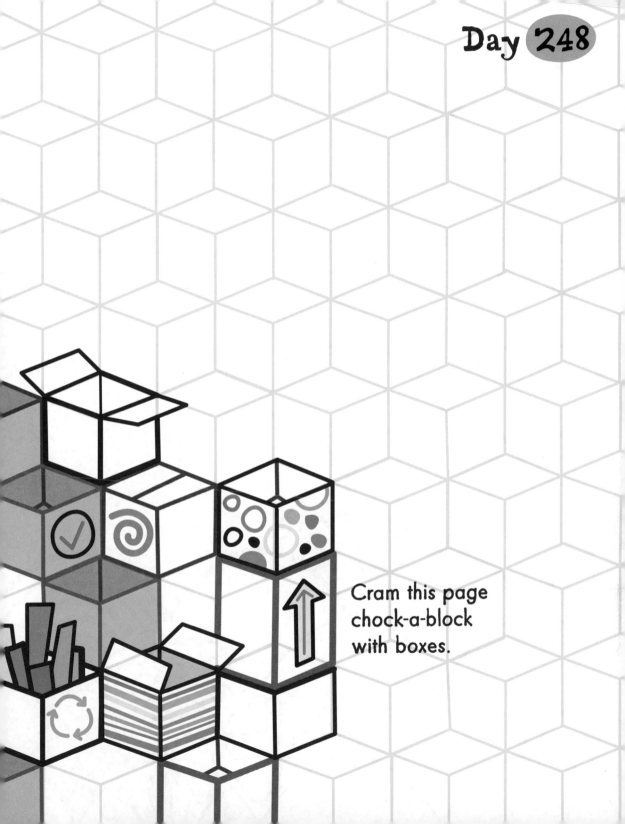

Cram this page chock-a-block with boxes.

Turn these curves into a magical landscape.

Cover the wall with twisting, thorny vines, and a few more bugs.

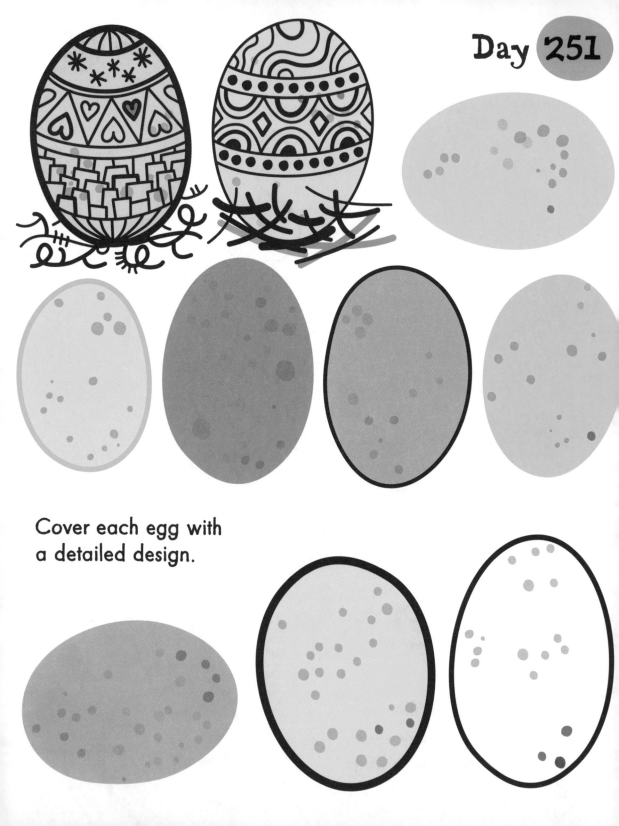

Cover each egg with
a detailed design.

Beep! Beep! Fill these roads with doodly traffic.

Complete the track to lead the train down the hillside.

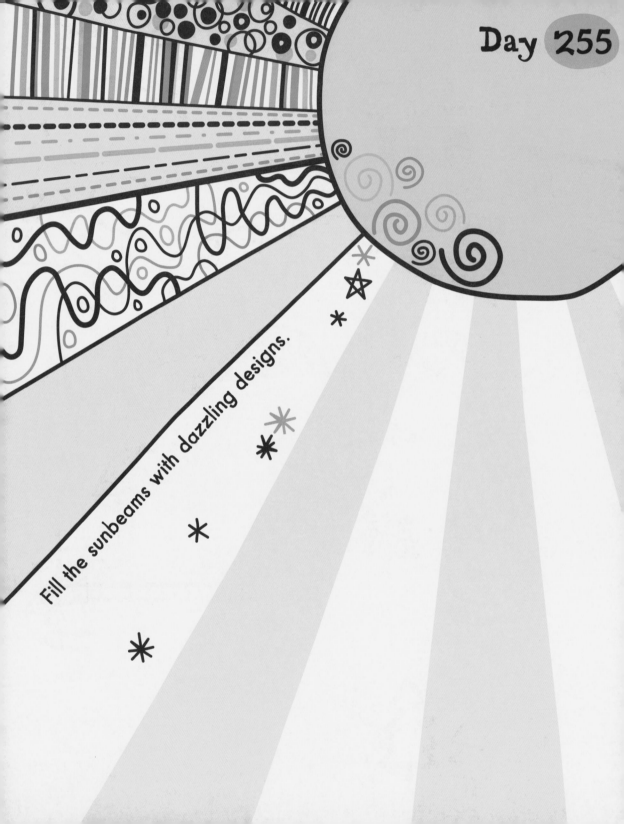

Fill the sunbeams with dazzling designs.

Day 256

Stitch doodly patterns onto each cushion.

Turn this rainbow rain into a feast of doodles.

Why not decorate some dinosaurs today?

Doodle more swirling spirals
and fill them with patterns.

Add your own style to these rings: fun, fancy and fabulous.

Draw lots more triangles today,
then fill them with doodles.

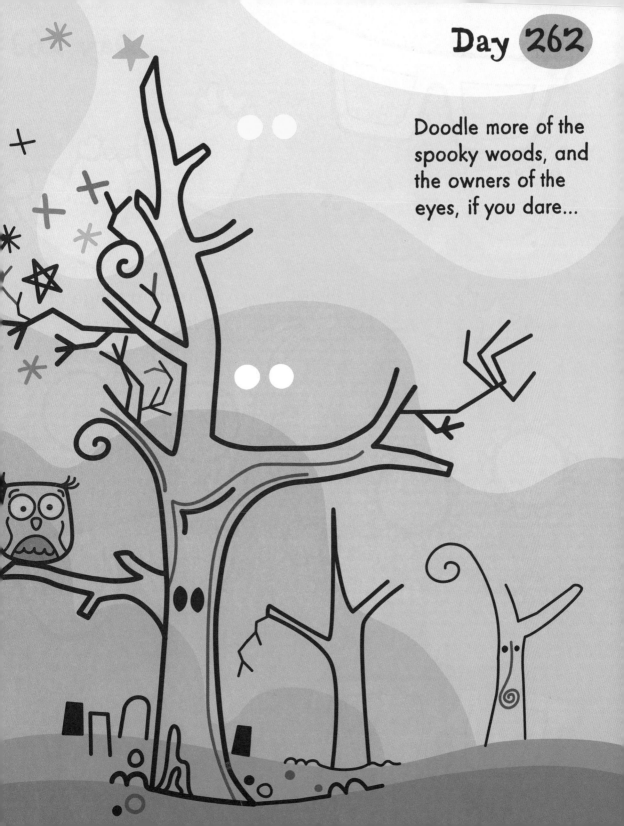

Doodle more of the spooky woods, and the owners of the eyes, if you dare...

Create a range of funky sunglasses.

Doodle more trees in this funny forest, and decorate them with unusual patterns.

Fill up these jars with sweet treats in tempting wrappers.

What other toys will
go on your shelves?

What will you dress up as today? Doodle more costumes.

Today, doodle all kinds
of things you might
find in a garden.

Add details and whirling sails to the windmills.

Doodle faces that make sense this way up...

...and this way up, too.

Give these candles cool designs and hot, dripping wax.

Day 272

Add tasteful patterns to the teacups.

Bugs and beetles come in all shapes and sizes, so doodle them as differently as you can.

Today, doodle stonework patterns on the castle walls and designs on the flags.

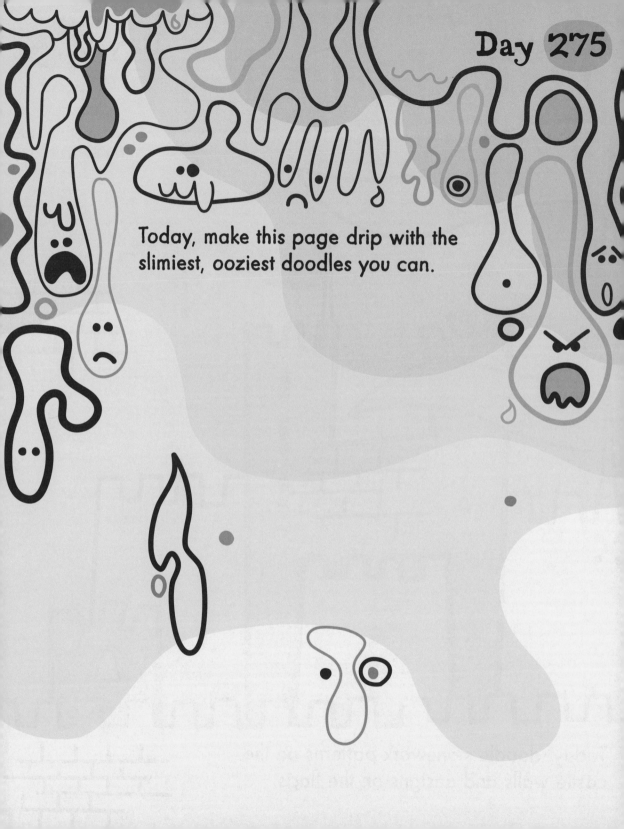

Day 275

Today, make this page drip with the slimiest, ooziest doodles you can.

Complete the cats' faces, then doodle some more.

Complete this work of modern art, then put it on display.

Cut or tear along this dotted line

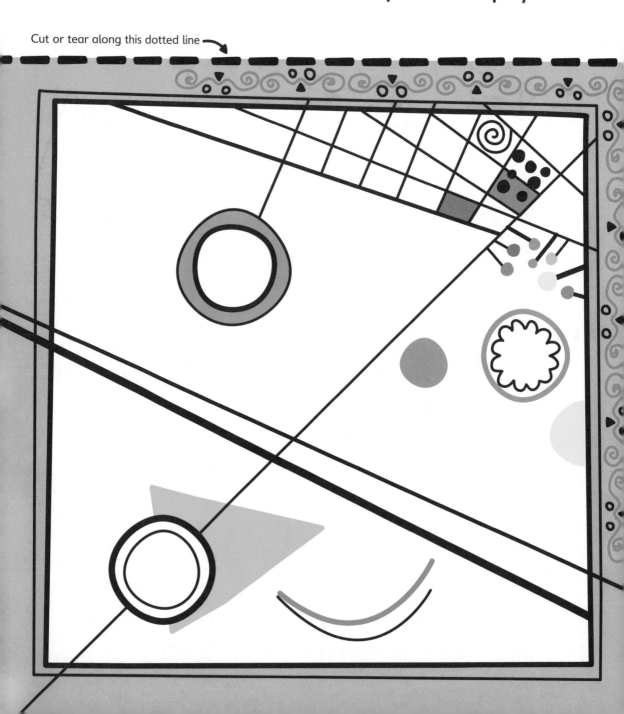

Jazz up
these ties with
dapper doodles.

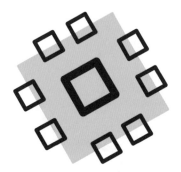

Doodle little
shapes all over
the big shapes.

Add patterns and rings to the planets,
and fill the page with moons and stars.

There's lots of room in the ants' nest. Add as many little black ants as you can.

Fill this page with
summery doodles.

Day 283

Fill this page with random doodles joined together.

space dust

Complete this page from an alien's scrapbook.

UFO FOR SALE

One alien owner from new, only 320 million light years on the clock. Has to be seen to be believed! zoog@

Doodle designs for some new flags.

DOODLES

Day 286

Draw dominoes with matching doodles where they touch.

Fill the page
with patterns
of hearts.

Complete the circuit so the red button wakes the robot up.

Doodle faces in the triangles.

Add eyes and markings to these tropical fish.

How many things can an oblong be?

Draw more cable cars and doodle some passengers.

Complete these
pictures as you wish.

Write on these gift tags
and doodle some more.

Fill the bath with bubbles
and decorated ducks.

Throw some more tasty food on the barbecue.

Day 298

What can you make out of these squashy little squares?

Design some invitations for
your perfect celebrations.

To: my friend
....

Let's CELEBRATE!..........

To:
....

For:
....

Make this volcano erupt with rivers of bubbling lava and flying rocks.

Turn these fruits into a crowd of funny faces.

What would you love to have? Make a list and doodle some illustrations.

- Trip into space!
- A butterfly farm
- A pet dinosaur

Add doodles to illustrate this recipe for a magic potion.

★ 3 grinning pumpkins

I rabbit whisker

A snail's silver slime

2 dragon teeth

I spider web

A pinch of pigeon poo

Today, design a brand new set of stamps.

Why not design your own
cover for this book?

Continue this
pattern with
flowery doodles.

Be a doodle dinosaur hunter
and dig up some more bones.

Plant more palm trees
on the islands, with
coconuts drifting
in the waves.

Add more shapes, lines and patterns
to create a work of modern art.

It's party time! Doodle some jolly patterns on the flags.

Today, the Bank of Bongolia has hired you to design their new coins and paper money. What will it look like?

Give these chameleons twisty tongues and pretty patterns – and add more tasty bugs.

Sunrise

Doodle Chain

Add some more doodles, with titles, to this gallery.

Doodle flickering flames and swirling smoke on the bonfire.

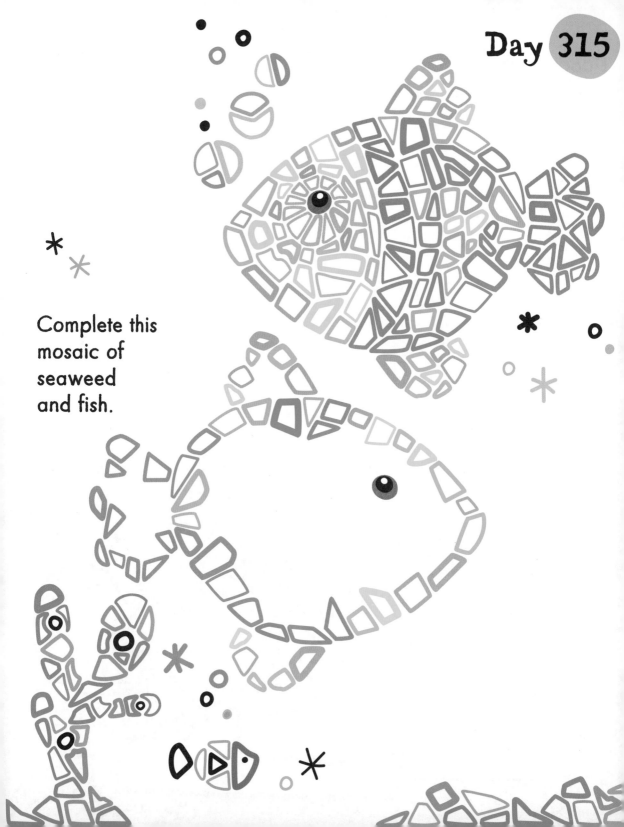

Complete this
mosaic of
seaweed
and fish.

Decorate the trucks
and doodle what
they're carrying.

Join up the pipes to pump the water up to the spout.

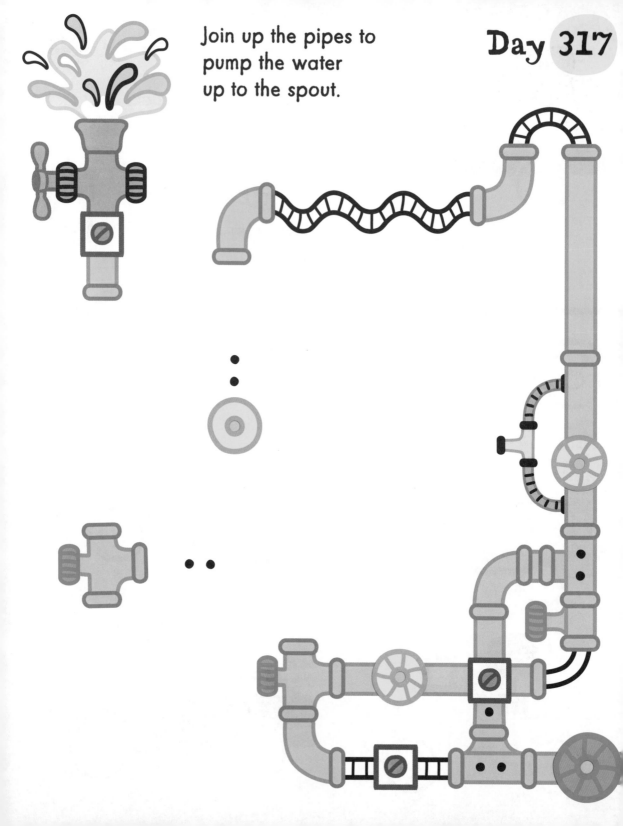

The castle is under attack!
Add lots more arrows and
plant a few trees where
soldiers can hide.

Half a circle can turn into anything – what will you make?

Doodle what's above
the ground...

...and what's
underground too.

Complete the aliens in doodly style.

See how many mini-motors
you can doodle on each line.

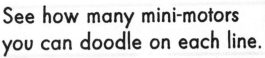

Continue the square spirals across the page.

Decorate the piggy
bank and coins
with your doodles.

Doodle some masks for an elegant ball.

Add more blossoms
to the branches.

Continue the
patterns on
these rugs.

Today, feed these Venus flytraps with yummy bugs.

Doodle on these
fabulous fungi, then
form a few more.

Doodle some things that
are lying around your room.

Dozens of tiny creatures live in this water drop, but there's room for you to doodle some more.

Day 331

Doodle some more stick people playing sports.

Day 333

Continue this muddy, leafy camouflage pattern across the page.

Illustrate this comic strip and decide how it ends.

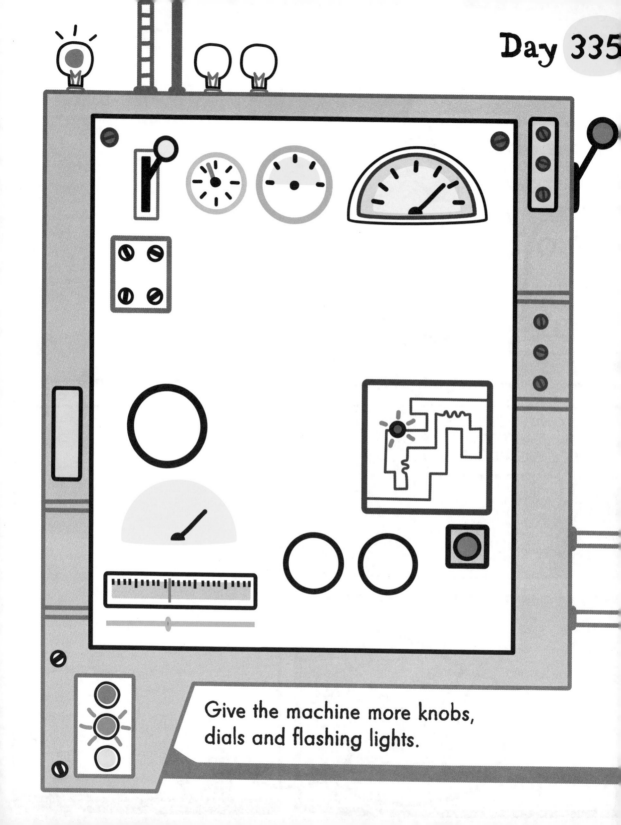

Give the machine more knobs, dials and flashing lights.

Complete the parachutes with lines, patterns, names — and people!

Give these shields bold designs fit for noble knights.

Doodle letters and numbers
jumbled together.

Doodle some memories
from yesterday...

...and the day
before that...

...and the day
before that, too.

Today, draw skiers, trees and cottages on these snowy hills.

Meow

Turn these punctuation marks
and signs into doodly designs.

Space can be a crowded place. Complete these alien spaceships.

Doodle patterns on the peas and pods.

Draw more bottles bobbing on the waves, with a doodly message in each one.

Doodle more spooks and add terrifying touches to the haunted house.

ROAR!

WOOF!

Day 346

Make each shape into a doodle animal.

Doodle your own designs to brighten up the clothes on the line.

Today, try turning these
handprints into doodles.

Complete the top doodle, then try to mirror it exactly below.

Continue the mysterious picture-writing on this ancient scroll.

Brighten up this
flowery pattern with
doodly decorations.

Turn these scribbles into doodles.

Day 353

Add scales and patterns to the fleeing fish, and a few more teeth to the hungry shark.

For today's doodle, turn this page into a galaxy of funky stars.

Today, doodle more germs and other teensy beasties.

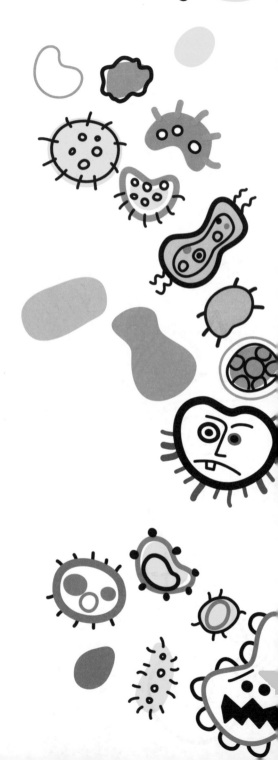

Doodle a few more fruits on the Everyfruit tree.

The magic lamp will grant
all the wishes you doodle...

Draw the rest of
Doodleville, with
houses, trees
and roads.

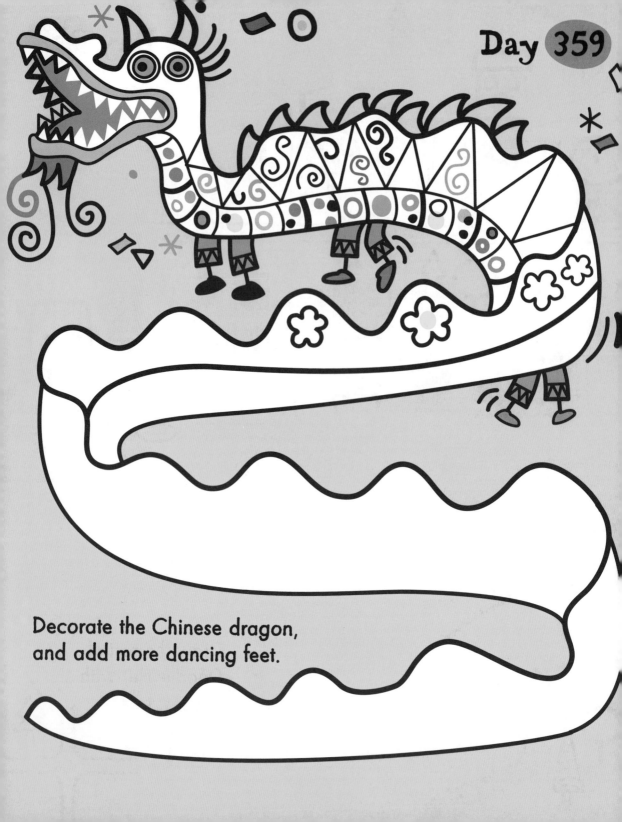

Decorate the Chinese dragon,
and add more dancing feet.

Hang up twinkly lights for a sparkling celebration.

Lots **of rotten** eggs

Smelly socks

Fresh snot

Eyeballs

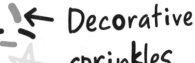

Decorative
sprinkles

Poisonous
toadstools

Continue these square spirals, then doodle inside them.

Doodle more ice-blocks to finish the igloos, and build another.

Make a little
world all of
your own.

Design a poster for an exhibition of your doodles.